Lebanon

📍 Beirut
📍 Burj el-Barajneh

✈ Beirut-Rafic Hariri International Airport

Recipes from a Refugee Food Truck

© 2017 Rebelhouse Publishing
All rights reserved

No part of this book may be reproduced, transmitted, or distributed in any form without written permission.

www.rebelhouse.com

President, Rebelhouse Publishing: Trevor Hall
Creative Director: Gretchen Thomas
Photography: Vivien Killilea Best
Book Design and Layout: Nickie DeTolve
Recipe Editor and Advisor: Rachel Best
Recipe Tester: Pat Whyde
Copy Editor: Jamie Feldmar
Photo Credit: Sarah Hunter, page 3

Printed In Canada | Hemlock Printers Ltd.

For the Women of Soufra

Left To Right

Abeer Masri عبير المصري Safeye Naser صفية ناصر Maha Hajjaj مهى هجاج
Ghada Masrieh غادة مصرية Mariam Shaar مريم الشعار Manal Hasan منال حسن
Ameera Fnesh أميرة فنيش Samar Hanafi سمر الحنفي

Not Present

Zeinab Jammal زينب جمال Randa Abbas رندة عباس Manal Faour منال فاعور
Diala Taleb ديالا طالب Mayssa Hussein ميساء حسين Samar Shaar سمر الشعار
Samia Ibrahim سامية ابراهيم Nehmat Al Zoghbi نعمة الزعبي Khadeja Abo Hassan خديجة ابو حسان

Mariam Shaar

This cookbook, and the affiliated documentary film also titled Soufra, by Rebelhouse Group, accompanies Mariam Shaar on her journey of empowerment by developing a thriving business that employs the incredible women of the Burj el-Barajneh refugee camp in Lebanon.

Mariam was born in the Burj el-Barajneh camp in the 1970s, almost three decades after her grandmother arrived as the Palestinian refugee crisis began. Like all refugees, her family was forbidden from holding most jobs, lacked documentation to leave the country legally, and did not have the financial means to move outside the camp. So they stayed. Mariam has spent her entire life in the camp, surviving the Lebanese Civil War and a series of other brutal conflicts, including the "war of the camps." Driven by a relentless desire to make life in the camp better, she dedicated herself to improving not only her own life but also the lives of those around her. In the 1990s, she joined the Women's Program Association, a community-based organization founded with the support of UNRWA to bring together women in the refugee camps in Lebanon to build new opportunities. Today she is the director of WPA's community-based center in the Burj el-Barajneh camp.

Mariam's vision has always been to create opportunities for the refugee community and improve lives through education and production. With the intention of creating a sustainable business at the WPA center in Burj el-Barajneh, she surveyed local women to get a sense of their interests. She discovered that many women were interested in utilizing their cooking skills, as they could participate in that at both the community center and in their own homes. Perhaps most important, it was something that reflected their heritage and passions, and something for which there would always be a market. Everyone needs to eat!

With seed funding and business planning support from Alfanar venture philanthropy, Soufra catering was born in 2013. Like any start-up, it went through many iterations. Different names, logos, and business plans were tested. Mariam partnered with Souk El Tayeb, a leading social enterprise in Lebanon, on training and branding. The idea was to revive traditional Palestinian dishes and offer them to the Beirut market. The dishes were met with huge acclaim. But despite the positive reviews, not enough catering orders were coming in. In a brainstorming session with the women of Soufra and its stakeholders, the idea of a food truck was hatched, and with it a whole new journey began!

In 2015, social justice filmmaker Thomas Morgan heard about Alfanar's work with Soufra. He came to Lebanon to meet Mariam, and ended up dedicating two years of his life to filming her story and helping turn her vision into reality. With the help of a Kickstarter campaign, the Soufra women raised more than enough money to launch the first-ever refugee food truck. In so doing, they made it possible to take their food and their business to customers all over Lebanon, and began providing more and more jobs for women inside the camp.

For the Children

This cookbook not only shares some of the most treasured recipes that changed the lives of the Soufra women, it will also help support families at the camp. The women of Soufra, through WPA, are full partners in the publication of this book. They will share equally in proceeds from its sales, which will support the ongoing development of the camp's Children's Center school.

Table of Contents

SAVORY (15)

Dolmas 16
Fatayer Fallahy 18
Msakhan 20
Tomato Jam 22
Sambousek 24
Muhammara 26
Pickled Cucumbers 28
Man'oushé 30
Potato Kibbeh 32
Molokhia 34
Chickpea Fatteh 36
Romanieh 38
Tabouli 40
Chicken Freekeh 42
Chicken Mansaf 44
Meat Mansaf 46
Qidra 48
Wheatberry Porridge 50

SWEET (55)

Maakaroun 56
Knafeh Nabulsieh 58
Molasses Cookies 60
Chocolate Balls 62
Makrouta 64
Coconut Namoura 66
Strawberry Tart 68
Pineapple Jam 70

Life In And Around
The Camp 75

Acknowledgements 93

Abeer Masri — "Dolmas are my favorite. I remember rolling the grape leaves with my sister and mother when I was a child."

عبير المصري المحاشي هي طبقي المفضل. أتذكر لفّ أوراق العنب مع أختي وأمي عندما كنت طفلة.

Samia Ibrahim — "I am from Syria and I love working in the kitchen, this is why I joined Soufra. My favorite dish is Makloubeh and among my favorite spices is finely ground red pepper."

سامية ابراهيم انا من سوريا احب مجال الطبخ كثير ولهذا السبب انضممت الى مطبخ سفرة. اكلتي المفضلة المقلوبة ومن البهارات احب الفلفل والحر المطحون

Diala Taleb — "I am from Iraq, married to a Palestinian. I love food and I have a lot of experience in this field. Stuffed squash is my favorite and I love all spices."

ديالا طالب انا امرأة عراقية متزوجة فلسطيني احب الطعام كثيرا ولدي خبرة في هذا المجال اجيد حشي الكوسى واحب البهارات

Savory

Ghada Masrieh — "I like the flavor of Sumac. One of my greatest joys is cooking with "Soufra" because I experience true happiness when preparing food for others. I like to make others happy by offering them delicious food."

غادة مصرية أنا أحب نكهة السمّاق. ومن دواعي سعادتي أن أطبخ مع "سفره" لأني أشعر بسعادة حقيقية عندما أصنع الطعام للآخرين. أنا أحبّ أن أُسعد الآخرين بأن أقدّم لهم طعاماً جيداً.

ورق عنب بخضرة

Dolmas (Stuffed Grape Leaves)

½ cup (120 g) grape leaves
1 ½ cup (297 g) white rice
1 bunch parsley
¼ bunch mint
1 small bunch green onions
2 pounds (1 kg) tomato
1 cup fresh-squeezed lemon juice (from 10-12 lemons), divided
1 cup (240 ml) olive oil
Salt and pepper to taste

4 large carrots
2 medium potatoes
2 medium yellow onions
2 medium tomatoes

If using canned leaves, boil leaves in salted water for 3 minutes. Drain and allow to cool. If using fresh leaves, boil in salted water until the leaves darken and become soft, about 1 minute. Drain and allow to cool.

Wash the rice and drain well. Finely chop the parsley, mint, green onion and tomato. Place chopped ingredients into a bowl along with the washed rice. Add half of the lemon juice, all of the olive oil and season mixture with salt and pepper.

Scoop a little of the mixture onto each grape leaf and roll tightly, tucking the ends of the leaf in to create a secure roll.

Cut the carrots, potatoes, onions and tomatoes into ¼-inch rounds. Place at the bottom of a large pot or saucepan. Lay the stuffed, rolled leaves on top of the vegetables. Pour enough salted water into the pot to just cover all ingredients.

Simmer, covered, for about 1 hour or until rice is cooked through. When cooked, add the rest of the lemon juice to the pot and serve.

Serves 6-8

فطاير فلاحي--زعتر بري

Fatayer Fallahy--Wild Thyme

Dough

1 cup water

4 cups (452 g) whole wheat flour

Pinch of salt

1 teaspoon (5 g) yeast

2 tablespoons (30 g) milk powder

Pinch of sugar

1 cup (240 ml) olive oil

Filling

2 yellow onions, diced small

1 bunch wild za'atar or dried za'atar if fresh is not available, chopped (Note: in this recipe za'atar is not the za'atar spice mix, but rather the leaves of fresh or dried thyme)

1 tablespoon fresh lemon juice

Olive oil as needed

Pinch of sumac

Make the dough: Heat the water until slightly warm. In a large bowl, combine the flour, salt, yeast, milk powder and sugar. Gradually add the water, mix well to form a uniform dough, and set aside for 30-45 minutes to rise.

In a large bowl, mix all the filling ingredients and set aside.

Once the dough has doubled in size, divide the ball into 3 pieces. Roll each of them on a surface greased with olive oil, rolling out until you make a paper-thin sheet of dough. Another option is to use your hands to press down and stretch the dough until it becomes very thin.

When the sheets are very thin, add a pinch of za'atar filling, then fold two sides of the dough to the middle. Add another pinch of za'atar filling and fold again. Keep adding pinches of za'atar and folding the dough another 3-4 times, creating a square pie. Set aside and rest for 10 minutes.

Preheat the oven to 350°F (180°C). Arrange pies on a baking sheet and bake for 10 minutes, or until slightly golden. Flip the pies over and bake for another 5 minutes, or until golden brown.

Makes 12 pies

Msakhan

1/3 cup (40 g) chopped almonds and/or pine nuts, toasted

2 pounds (1 kg) chicken thighs

4 tablespoons olive oil, plus more for drizzling

4 large onions, finely diced

1/3 cup (80 g) sumac

1 teaspoon (5 g) allspice

½ teaspoon (2 g) black pepper

Salt to taste

Saj bread (thin pita) or lavash

Add the chicken to a large stockpot and cover with water. Bring to a boil, then reduce to a simmer and cook for about 45 minutes, or until chicken is tender and meat easily pulls away from the bone. Remove from water, and when chicken is cool enough to handle, remove skin and bones, and cut meat into bite-sized pieces.

Heat olive oil in a large sauté pan over medium heat. Add onions and cook until golden brown, 12-15 minutes. Add sumac, allspice, black pepper and salt, then add the chicken pieces and stir well to combine.

Add the almonds and pine nuts and set aside to cool.

Preheat oven to 350°F (180°C).

Cut each saj bread into 6 triangular pieces. Place a spoonful of chicken mixture at the base of the triangle and roll the base to the point, forming a little cigar. Set cigars on baking sheet and drizzle with olive oil. Bake for about 10 minutes or until golden brown.

Makes approximately 100 rolls

Form W-2 Wage and Tax Statement 2021

Copy C, for employee's records

d Control number: 0902-14117347 / 0000000066 - DEPT 1	Department of the Treasury - Internal Revenue Service / OMB No. 1545-0008
b Employer identification number (EIN): 06-0904040	a Employee's social security number: XXX-XX-6281
c Employer's name, address, and ZIP code: ONE STRAWBERRY HILL CONDO ASSO, 1010 HOPE ST, STAMFORD CT 06907	
1 Wages, tips, other compensation: 21420.00	2 Federal income tax withheld: 1383.54
3 Social security wages: 21420.00	4 Social security tax withheld: 1328.04
5 Medicare wages and tips: 21420.00	6 Medicare tax withheld: 310.59
7 Social Security Tips:	8 Allocated Tips:
10 Dependent care benefits:	11 Nonqualified plans:
12 See instructions for box 12:	14 Other: CTPFL 107.10
13 Statutory employee / Retirement plan / Third-party sick pay	
e Employee's name, address, and ZIP code: ROBENSON JEAN CHARLES, 35 W BROAD ST, APT. # 221, STAMFORD CT 06902	
15 State: CT	Employer's state ID number: 1094630-000
16 State wages, tips, etc.: 21420.00	17 State income tax: 712.33
18 Local wages, tips, etc.:	19 Local income tax:	20 Locality name:

This information is being furnished to the Internal Revenue Service. If you are required to file a tax return, a negligence penalty or other sanction may be imposed on you if this income is taxable and you fail to report it.

Form W-2 Wage and Tax Statement 2021

Copy B, to be filed with employee's FEDERAL tax return

d Control number: 0902-14117347 / 0000000066 - DEPT 1	Department of the Treasury - Internal Revenue Service / OMB No. 1545-0008
b Employer identification number (EIN): 06-0904040	a Employee's social security number: XXX-XX-6281
c Employer's name, address, and ZIP code: ONE STRAWBERRY HILL CONDO ASSO, 1010 HOPE ST, STAMFORD CT 06907	
1 Wages, tips, other compensation: 21420.00	2 Federal income tax withheld: 1383.54
3 Social security wages: 21420.00	4 Social security tax withheld: 1328.04
5 Medicare wages and tips: 21420.00	6 Medicare tax withheld: 310.59
7 Social Security Tips:	8 Allocated Tips:
10 Dependent care benefits:	11 Nonqualified plans:
12 See instructions for box 12:	14 Other: CTPFL 107.10
13 Statutory employee / Retirement plan / Third-party sick pay	
e Employee's name, address, and ZIP code: ROBENSON JEAN CHARLES, 35 W BROAD ST, APT. # 221, STAMFORD CT 06902	
15 State: CT	Employer's state ID number: 1094630-000
16 State wages, tips, etc.: 21420.00	17 State income tax: 712.33
18 Local wages, tips, etc.:	19 Local income tax:	20 Locality name:

This information is being furnished to the Internal Revenue Service. If you are required to file a tax return, a negligence penalty or other sanction may be imposed on you if this income is taxable and you fail to report it.

Form W-2 Wage and Tax Statement 2021

Copy 2, to be filed with employee's tax return for CT

d Control number: 0902-14117347 / 0000000066 - DEPT 1	Department of the Treasury - Internal Revenue Service / OMB No. 1545-0008
b Employer identification number (EIN): 06-0904040	a Employee's social security number: XXX-XX-6281
c Employer's name, address, and ZIP code: ONE STRAWBERRY HILL CONDO ASSO, 1010 HOPE ST, STAMFORD CT 06907	
1 Wages, tips, other compensation: 21420.00	2 Federal income tax withheld: 1383.54
3 Social security wages: 21420.00	4 Social security tax withheld: 1328.04
5 Medicare wages and tips: 21420.00	6 Medicare tax withheld: 310.59
7 Social Security Tips:	8 Allocated Tips:
10 Dependent care benefits:	11 Nonqualified plans:
12 See instructions for box 12:	14 Other: CTPFL 107.10
13 Statutory employee / Retirement plan / Third-party sick pay	
e Employee's name, address, and ZIP code: ROBENSON JEAN CHARLES, 35 W BROAD ST, APT. # 221, STAMFORD CT 06902	
15 State: CT	Employer's state ID number: 1094630-000
16 State wages, tips, etc.: 21420.00	17 State income tax: 712.33
18 Local wages, tips, etc.:	19 Local income tax:	20 Locality name:

This information is being furnished to the Internal Revenue Service. If you are required to file a tax return, a negligence penalty or other sanction may be imposed on you if this income is taxable and you fail to report it.

Form W-2 Wage and Tax Statement 2021

d Control number:	Void: X
b Employer identification number (EIN):	a Employee's social security number:
c Employer's name, address, and ZIP code:	Department of the Treasury - Internal Revenue Service / OMB No. 1545-0008
1 Wages, tips, other compensation:	2 Federal income tax withheld:
3 Social security wages:	4 Social security tax withheld:
5 Medicare wages and tips:	6 Medicare tax withheld:
7 Social Security Tips:	8 Allocated Tips:
10 Dependent care benefits:	11 Nonqualified plans:
12 See instructions for box 12:	14 Other:
13 Statutory employee / Retirement plan / Third-party sick pay	
e Employee's name, address, and ZIP code:	
15 State:	Employer's state ID number:
16 State wages, tips, etc.:	17 State income tax:
18 Local wages, tips, etc.:	19 Local income tax:	20 Locality name:

This information is being furnished to the Internal Revenue Service. If you are required to file a tax return, a negligence penalty or other sanction may be imposed on you if this income is taxable and you fail to report it.

TO OPEN - SEE REVERSE SIDE

PRESORTED
FIRST-CLASS MAIL
U.S. POSTAGE
PAID
GREEN BAY, WI
PERMIT NO. 431

ONE STRAWBERRY HILL CONDO ASSO
1010 HOPE ST
STAMFORD CT 06907

ADDRESS SERVICE REQUESTED

Dept. Number: DEPT 1

01/07/22

IMPORTANT TAX RETURN DOCUMENTS ENCLOSED

ROBENSON JEAN CHARLES
35 W BROAD ST
APT. # 221
STAMFORD CT 06902

2021 W-2 and EARNINGS SUMMARY

Employee Reference Copy
W-2 Wage and Tax Statement 2021
Copy C for employee's records. OMB No. 1545-0008

Control number	Dept.	Corp.	Employer use only
000069576 NMY	2494A3	BUV1	A S 220418

Employer's name, address, and ZIP code
ACME MARKETS INC
PO BOX 52131
PHOENIX, AZ 85072-2131

e/f Employee's name, address, and ZIP code
ROBENSON JEAN CHARLES
35 W BROAD ST APT 221
STAMFORD, CT 06902

b Employer's FED ID number	a Employee's SSA number
87-0440072	XXX-XX-6281

Box	Description	Amount
1	Wages, tips, other comp.	4275.76
2	Federal income tax withheld	28.19
3	Social security wages	4275.76
4	Social security tax withheld	265.10
5	Medicare wages and tips	4275.76
6	Medicare tax withheld	62.00
7	Social security tips	
8	Allocated tips	
10	Dependent care benefits	
11	Nonqualified plans	
12a	See instructions for box 12	
14	Other	21.38 CT PFL

13 Stat emp. | Ret. plan | 3rd party sick pay

15 State	Employer's state ID no.	16 State wages, tips, etc.
CT	51399582-000	4275.76
17 State income tax	.08	18 Local wages, tips, etc.
19 Local income tax		20 Locality name

ROBENSON JEAN CHARLES
35 W BROAD ST APT 221
STAMFORD, CT 06902

Social Security Number: XXX-XX-6281

© 2021 ADP, Inc.

PAGE 01 OF 01

Federal Filing Copy — W-2 Wage and Tax Statement 2021
Copy B to be filed with employee's Federal Income Tax Return. OMB No. 1545-0008

1	Wages, tips, other comp.	4275.76
2	Federal income tax withheld	28.19
3	Social security wages	4275.76
4	Social security tax withheld	265.10
5	Medicare wages and tips	4275.76
6	Medicare tax withheld	62.00

d Control number	Dept.	Corp.	Employer use only
0000069576 NMY	2494A3	BUV1	A 220418

ACME MARKETS INC
PO BOX 52131
PHOENIX, AZ 85072-2131

b Employer's FED ID number	a Employee's SSA number
87-0440072	XXX-XX-6281

14 Other 21.38 CT PFL

ROBENSON JEAN CHARLES
35 W BROAD ST APT 221
STAMFORD, CT 06902

15 State	Employer's state ID no.	16 State wages, tips, etc.
CT	51399582-000	4275.76
17 State income tax	.08	

CT. State Filing Copy — W-2 Wage and Tax Statement 2021
Copy 2 to be filed with employee's State Income Tax Return. OMB No. 1545-0008

(Same figures as above)

City or Local Filing Copy — W-2 Wage and Tax Statement 2021
Copy 2 to be filed with employee's City or Local Income Tax Return. OMB No. 1545-0008

(Same figures as above)

Instructions for Employee

Box 1. Enter this amount on the wages line of your tax return.

Box 2. Enter this amount on the federal income tax withheld line of your tax return.

Box 5. You may be required to report this amount on Form 8959, Additional Medicare Tax. See the Instructions for Forms 1040 and 1040-SR to determine if you are required to complete Form 8959.

Box 6. This amount includes the 1.45% Medicare Tax withheld on all Medicare wages and tips shown in box 5, as well as the 0.9% Additional Medicare Tax on any of those Medicare wages and tips above $200,000.

Box 8. This amount is **not** included in box 1, 3, 5, or 7. For information on how to report tips on your tax return, see the Instructions for Forms 1040 and 1040-SR.

You must file Form 4137, Social Security and Medicare Tax on Unreported Tip Income, with your income tax return to report at least the allocated tip amount unless you can prove with adequate records that you received a smaller amount. If you have records that show the actual amount of tips you received, report that amount even if it is more or less than the allocated tips. Use Form 4137 to figure the social security and Medicare tax owed on tips you didn't report to your employer. Enter this amount on the wages line of your tax return. By filing Form 4137, your social security tips will be credited to your social security record (used to figure your benefits).

Box 10. This amount includes the total dependent care benefits that your employer paid to or incurred on your behalf (including amounts from a section 125 (cafeteria) plan). Any amount over $5,000 is also included in box 1. Complete Form 2441, Child and Dependent Care Expenses, to figure any taxable and nontaxable amounts.

Box 11. This amount is (a) reported in box 1 if it is a distribution made to you from a nonqualified deferred compensation or nongovernmental section 457(b) plan, or (b) included in box 3 and/or box 5 if it is a prior year deferral under a nonqualified or section 457(b) plan that became taxable for social security and Medicare taxes this year because there is no longer a substantial risk of forfeiture of your right to the deferred amount. This box shouldn't be used if you had a deferral and a distribution in the same calendar year. If you made a deferral and received a distribution in the same calendar year, and you are or will be age 62 by the end of the calendar year, your employer should file Form SSA-131, Employer Report of Special Wage Payments, with the Social Security Administration and give you a copy.

Box 12. The following list explains the codes shown in box 12. You may need this information to complete your tax return. Elective deferrals (codes D, E, F, and S) and designated Roth contributions (codes AA, BB, and EE) under all plans are generally limited to a total of $19,500 ($13,500 if you only have SIMPLE plans; $22,500 for section 403(b) plans if you qualify for the 15-year rule explained in Pub. 571). Deferrals under code G are limited to $19,500. Deferrals under code H are limited to $7,000.

However, if you were at least age 50 in 2021, your employer may have allowed an additional deferral of up to $6,500 ($3,000 for section 401(k)(11) and 408(p) SIMPLE plans). This additional deferral amount is not subject to the overall limit on elective deferrals. For code G, the limit on elective deferrals may be higher for the last 3 years before you reach retirement age. Contact your plan administrator for more information. Amounts in excess of the overall elective deferral limit must be included in income. See the Instructions for Forms 1040 and 1040-SR.

Note: If a year follows code D through H, S, Y, AA, BB, or EE, you made a make-up pension contribution for a prior year(s) when you were in military service. To figure whether you made excess deferrals, consider these amounts for the year shown, not the current year. If no year is shown, the contributions are for the current year.

A—Uncollected social security or RRTA tax on tips. Include this tax on Form 1040 or 1040-SR. See the Instructions for Forms 1040 and 1040-SR.

B—Uncollected Medicare tax on tips. Include this tax on Form 1040 or 1040-SR. See the Instructions for Forms 1040 and 1040-SR.

C—Taxable cost of group-term life insurance over $50,000 (included in boxes 1, 3 (up to the social security wage base), and 5)

D—Elective deferrals to a section 401(k) cash or deferred arrangement. Also includes deferrals under a SIMPLE retirement account that is part of a section 401(k) arrangement.

E—Elective deferrals under a section 403(b) salary reduction agreement

F—Elective deferrals under a section 408(k)(6) salary reduction SEP

G—Elective deferrals and employer contributions (including nonelective deferrals) to a section 457(b) deferred compensation plan

H—Elective deferrals to a section 501(c)(18)(D) tax-exempt organization plan. See the Instructions for Forms 1040 and 1040-SR for how to deduct.

J—Nontaxable sick pay (information only, not included in box 1, 3, or 5)

K—20% excise tax on excess golden parachute payments. See the Instructions for Forms 1040 and 1040-SR.

L—Substantiated employee business expense reimbursements (nontaxable)

M—Uncollected social security or RRTA tax on taxable cost of group-term life insurance over $50,000 (former employees only). See the Instructions for Forms 1040 and 1040-SR.

N—Uncollected Medicare tax on taxable cost of group-term life insurance over $50,000 (former employees only). See the Instructions for Forms 1040 and 1040-SR.

P—Excludable moving expense reimbursements paid directly to a member of the U.S. Armed Forces (not included in box 1, 3, or 5)

Q—Nontaxable combat pay. See the Instructions for Forms 1040 and 1040-SR for details on reporting this amount.

R—Employer contributions to your Archer MSA. Report on Form 8853, Archer MSAs and Long-Term Care Insurance Contracts.

S—Employee salary reduction contributions under a section 408(p) SIMPLE plan (not included in box 1)

T—Adoption benefits (not included in box 1). Complete Form 8839, Qualified Adoption Expenses, to figure any taxable and nontaxable amounts.

V—Income from exercise of nonstatutory stock option(s) (included in boxes 1, 3 (up to the social security wage base), and 5). See Pub. 525, Taxable and Nontaxable Income, for reporting requirements.

W—Employer contributions (including amounts the employee elected to contribute using a section 125 (cafeteria) plan) to your health savings account. Report on Form 8889, Health Savings Accounts (HSAs).

Y—Deferrals under a section 409A nonqualified deferred compensation plan

Z—Income under a nonqualified deferred compensation plan that fails to satisfy section 409A. This amount is also included in box 1. It is subject to an additional 20% tax plus interest. See the Instructions for Forms 1040 and 1040-SR.

AA—Designated Roth contributions under a section 401(k) plan

BB—Designated Roth contributions under a section 403(b) plan

DD—Cost of employer-sponsored health coverage. **The amount reported with code DD is not taxable.**

EE—Designated Roth contributions under a governmental section 457(b) plan. This amount does not apply to contributions under a tax-exempt organization section 457(b) plan.

FF—Permitted benefits under a qualified small employer health reimbursement arrangement

GG—Income from qualified equity grants under section 83(i)

HH—Aggregate deferrals under section 83(i) elections as of the close of the calendar year

Box 13. If the "Retirement plan" box is checked, special limits may apply to the amount of traditional IRA contributions you may deduct. See Pub. 590-A, Contributions to Individual Retirement Arrangements (IRAs).

Box 14. Employers may use this box to report information such as state disability insurance taxes withheld, union dues, uniform payments, health insurance premiums deducted, nontaxable income, educational assistance payments, or a member of the clergy's parsonage allowance and utilities. Railroad employers use this box to report railroad retirement (RRTA) compensation, Tier 1 tax, Tier 2 tax, Medicare tax, and Additional Medicare Tax. Include tips reported by the employee to the employer in railroad retirement (RRTA) compensation.

Note: Keep **Copy C** of Form W-2 for at least 3 years after the due date for filing your income tax return. However, to help **protect your social security benefits**, keep Copy C until you begin receiving social security benefits, just in case there is a question about your work record and/or earnings in a particular year.

Department of the Treasury - Internal Revenue Service

NOTE: THESE ARE SUBSTITUTE WAGE AND TAX STATEMENTS AND ARE ACCEPTABLE FOR FILING WITH YOUR FEDERAL, STATE AND LOCAL/CITY INCOME TAX RETURNS.

This information is being furnished to the Internal Revenue Service. If you are required to file a tax return, a negligence penalty or other sanction may be imposed on you if this income is taxable and you fail to report it.

IMPORTANT NOTE:

In order to insure efficient processing, attach this W-2 to your tax return like this (following agency instructions):

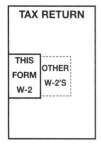

Notice to Employee

Do you have to file? Refer to the Instructions for Forms 1040 and 1040-SR to determine if you are required to file a tax return. Even if you don't have to file a tax return, you may be eligible for a refund if box 2 shows an amount or if you are eligible for any credit.

Earned income credit (EIC). You may be able to take the EIC for 2021 if your adjusted gross income (AGI) is less than a certain amount. The amount of the credit is based on income and family size. Workers without children could qualify for a smaller credit. You and any qualifying children must have valid social security numbers (SSNs). You can't take the EIC if your investment income is more than the specified amount for 2021 or if income is earned for services provided while you were an inmate at a penal institution. For 2021 income limits and more information, visit *www.irs.gov/EITC*. See also Pub. 596, Earned Income Credit. **Any EIC that is more than your tax liability is refunded to you, but only if you file a tax return.**

Employee's social security number (SSN). For your protection, this form may show only the last four digits of your SSN. However, your employer has reported your complete SSN to the IRS and SSA.

Clergy and religious workers. If you aren't subject to social security and Medicare taxes, see Pub. 517, Social Security and Other Information for Members of the Clergy and Religious Workers.

Corrections. If your name, SSN, or address is incorrect, correct Copies B, C, and 2 and ask your employer to correct your employment record. Be sure to ask the employer to file Form W-2c, Corrected Wage and Tax Statement, with the Social Security Administration (SSA) to correct any name, SSN, or money amount error reported to the SSA on Form W-2. Be sure to get your copies of Form W-2c from your employer for all corrections made so you may file them with your tax return. If your name and SSN are correct but aren't the same as shown on your social security card, you should ask for a new card that displays your correct name at any SSA office or by calling 800-772-1213. You may also visit the SSA website at *www.SSA.gov*.

Cost of employer-sponsored health coverage (if such cost is provided by the employer). The reporting in box 12, using code DD, of the cost of employer-sponsored health coverage is for your information only. **The amount reported with code DD is not taxable.**

Credit for excess taxes. If you had more than one employer in 2021 and more than $8,853.60 in social security and/or Tier 1 railroad retirement (RRTA) taxes were withheld, you may be able to claim a credit for the excess against your federal income tax. If you had more than one railroad employer and more than $5,203.80 in Tier 2 RRTA tax was withheld, you may also be able to claim a credit. See the Instructions for Forms 1040 and 1040-SR and Pub. 505, Tax Withholding and Estimated Tax.

Department of the Treasury - Internal Revenue Service

Department of the Treasury - Internal Revenue Service

2021 W-2 and EARNINGS SUMMARY

Employee Reference Copy

W-2 Wage and Tax Statement 2021
Copy C for employee's records. OMB No. 1545-0008

Control number	Dept.	Corp.	Employer use only
000112973 UNT	0624	BRA0	S 54563

Employer's name, address, and ZIP code
THE STOP & SHOP SUPERMARKET
COMPANY LLC
P.O. BOX 55836
PAYROLL DEPT.
BOSTON, MA 02205

Employee's name, address, and ZIP code
ROBENSON JEAN CHARLES
35 WEST BROAD ST
221 APT 221
STAMFORD, CT 06902

Employer's FED ID number	04-3061447	
a Employee's SSA number	XXX-XX-6281	
1 Wages, tips, other comp.		249.00
2 Federal income tax withheld		
3 Social security wages		249.00
4 Social security tax withheld		15.44
5 Medicare wages and tips		249.00
6 Medicare tax withheld		3.61
7 Social security tips		
8 Allocated tips		
10 Dependent care benefits		
11 Nonqualified plans		
12a See instructions for box 12		
14 Other	1.25 CT PFL	
12b		
12c		
12d		
13 Stat emp. Ret. plan 3rd party sick pay		

15 State	Employer's state ID no.	16 State wages, tips, etc.
CT	7188535-000	249.00
17 State income tax	17.40	
18 Local wages, tips, etc.		
19 Local income tax		
20 Locality name		

The wages, tips, and other compensation reflected in box 1 are the sum of those wages shown on your last pay statement, plus any additional compensation or adjustments received after the payroll close.

Your gross pay may not match your box 1 totals due to adjustments made for GTL, 401(k), cafeteria plans, etc...

To change your employee W-4 profile information, file a new W-4 with your payroll department.

ROBENSON JEAN CHARLES
35 WEST BROAD ST
221 APT 221
STAMFORD, CT 06902

Social Security Number: XXX-XX-6281

© 2021 ADP, Inc.

PAGE 01 OF 01

Federal Filing Copy

Box	Amount
1 Wages, tips, other comp.	249.00
2 Federal income tax withheld	
3 Social security wages	249.00
4 Social security tax withheld	15.44
5 Medicare wages and tips	249.00
6 Medicare tax withheld	3.61
d Control number	0000112973 UNT
Dept.	0624
Corp.	BRA0
Employer use only	54563

c Employer's name, address, and ZIP code
THE STOP & SHOP SUPERMARKET
COMPANY LLC
P.O. BOX 55836
PAYROLL DEPT.
BOSTON, MA 02205

b Employer's FED ID number: 04-3061447
a Employee's SSA number: XXX-XX-6281

7 Social security tips
8 Allocated tips
10 Dependent care benefits
11 Nonqualified plans
12a See instructions for box 12
14 Other 1.25 CT PFL
12b / 12c / 12d
13 Stat emp. Ret. plan 3rd party sick pay

e/f Employee's name, address and ZIP code
ROBENSON JEAN CHARLES
35 WEST BROAD ST
221 APT 221
STAMFORD, CT 06902

15 State CT Employer's state ID no. 7188535-000 16 State wages, tips, etc. 249.00
17 State income tax 17.40
18 Local wages, tips, etc.
19 Local income tax
20 Locality name

W-2 Wage and Tax Statement 2021
Copy B to be filed with employee's Federal Income Tax Return. OMB No. 1545-0008

CT. State Filing Copy

(Same box values as above — Wages 249.00; SS tax 15.44; Medicare tax 3.61; CT PFL 1.25; State wages 249.00; State income tax 17.40)

W-2 Wage and Tax Statement 2021
Copy 2 to be filed with employee's State Income Tax Return. OMB No. 1545-0008

City or Local Filing Copy

(Same box values as above)

W-2 Wage and Tax Statement 2021
Copy 2 to be filed with employee's City or Local Income Tax Return. OMB No. 1545-0008

Instructions for Employee

Box 1. Enter this amount on the wages line of your tax return.

Box 2. Enter this amount on the federal income tax withheld line of your tax return.

Box 5. You may be required to report this amount on Form 8959, Additional Medicare Tax. See the Instructions for Forms 1040 and 1040-SR to determine if you are required to complete Form 8959.

Box 6. This amount includes the 1.45% Medicare Tax withheld on all Medicare wages and tips shown in box 5, as well as the 0.9% Additional Medicare Tax on any of those Medicare wages and tips above $200,000.

Box 8. This amount is **not** included in box 1, 3, 5, or 7. For information on how to report tips on your tax return, see the Instructions for Forms 1040 and 1040-SR.

You must file Form 4137, Social Security and Medicare Tax on Unreported Tip Income, with your income tax return to report at least the allocated tip amount unless you can prove with adequate records that you received a smaller amount. If you have records that show the actual amount of tips you received, report that amount even if it is more or less than the allocated tips. Use Form 4137 to figure the social security and Medicare tax owed on tips you didn't report to your employer. Enter this amount on the wages line of your tax return. By filing Form 4137, your social security tips will be credited to your social security record (used to figure your benefits).

Box 10. This amount includes the total dependent care benefits that your employer paid to you or incurred on your behalf (including amounts from a section 125 (cafeteria) plan). Any amount over $5,000 is also included in box 1. Complete Form 2441, Child and Dependent Care Expenses, to figure any taxable and nontaxable amounts.

Box 11. This amount is (a) reported in box 1 if it is a distribution made to you from a nonqualified deferred compensation or nongovernmental section 457(b) plan, or (b) included in box 3 and/or box 5 if it is a prior year deferral under a nonqualified or section 457(b) plan that became taxable for social security and Medicare taxes this year because there is no longer a substantial risk of forfeiture of your right to the deferred amount. This box shouldn't be used if you had a deferral and a distribution in the same calendar year. If you made a deferral and received a distribution in the same calendar year, and you are or will be age 62 by the end of the calendar year, your employer should file Form SSA-131, Employer Report of Special Wage Payments, with the Social Security Administration and give you a copy.

Box 12. The following list explains the codes shown in box 12. You may need this information to complete your tax return. Elective deferrals (codes D, E, F, and S) and designated Roth contributions (codes AA, BB, and EE) under all plans are generally limited to a total of $19,500 ($13,500 if you only have SIMPLE plans; $22,500 for section 403(b) plans if you qualify for the 15-year rule explained in Pub. 571). Deferrals under code G are limited to $19,500. Deferrals under code H are limited to $7,000.

However, if you were at least age 50 in 2021, your employer may have allowed an additional deferral of up to $6,500 ($3,000 for section 401(k)(11) and 408(p) SIMPLE plans). This additional deferral amount is not subject to the overall limit on elective deferrals. For code G, the limit on elective deferrals may be higher for the last 3 years before you reach retirement age. Contact your plan administrator for more information. Amounts in excess of the overall elective deferral limit must be included in income. See the Instructions for Forms 1040 and 1040-SR.

Note: If a year follows code D through H, S, Y, AA, BB, or EE, you made a make-up pension contribution for a prior year(s) when you were in military service. To figure whether you made excess deferrals, consider these amounts for the year shown, not the current year. If no year is shown, the contributions are for the current year.

A—Uncollected social security or RRTA tax on tips. Include this tax on Form 1040 or 1040-SR. See the Instructions for Forms 1040 and 1040-SR.

B—Uncollected Medicare tax on tips. Include this tax on Form 1040 or 1040-SR. See the Instructions for Forms 1040 and 1040-SR.

C—Taxable cost of group-term life insurance over $50,000 (included in boxes 1, 3 (up to the social security wage base), and 5)

D—Elective deferrals to a section 401(k) cash or deferred arrangement. Also includes deferrals under a SIMPLE retirement account that is part of a section 401(k) arrangement.

E—Elective deferrals under a section 403(b) salary reduction agreement

F—Elective deferrals under a section 408(k)(6) salary reduction SEP

G—Elective deferrals and employer contributions (including nonelective deferrals) to a section 457(b) deferred compensation plan

H—Elective deferrals to a section 501(c)(18)(D) tax-exempt organization plan. See the Instructions for Forms 1040 and 1040-SR for how to deduct.

J—Nontaxable sick pay (information only, not included in box 1, 3, or 5)

K—20% excise tax on excess golden parachute payments. See the Instructions for Forms 1040 and 1040-SR.

L—Substantiated employee business expense reimbursements (nontaxable)

M—Uncollected social security or RRTA tax on taxable cost of group-term life insurance over $50,000 (former employees only). See the Instructions for Forms 1040 and 1040-SR.

N—Uncollected Medicare tax on taxable cost of group-term life insurance over $50,000 (former employees only). See the Instructions for Forms 1040 and 1040-SR.

P—Excludable moving expense reimbursements paid directly to a member of the U.S. Armed Forces (not included in box 1, 3, or 5)

Q—Nontaxable combat pay. See the Instructions for Forms 1040 and 1040-SR for details on reporting this amount.

R—Employer contributions to your Archer MSA. Report on Form 8853, Archer MSAs and Long-Term Care Insurance Contracts.

S—Employee salary reduction contributions under a section 408(p) SIMPLE plan (not included in box 1)

T—Adoption benefits (not included in box 1). Complete Form 8839, Qualified Adoption Expenses, to figure any taxable and nontaxable amounts.

V—Income from exercise of nonstatutory stock option(s) (included in boxes 1, 3 (up to the social security wage base), and 5). See Pub. 525, Taxable and Nontaxable Income, for reporting requirements.

W—Employer contributions (including amounts the employee elected to contribute using a section 125 (cafeteria) plan) to your health savings account. Report on Form 8889, Health Savings Accounts (HSAs).

Y—Deferrals under a section 409A nonqualified deferred compensation plan

Z—Income under a nonqualified deferred compensation plan that fails to satisfy section 409A. This amount is also included in box 1. It is subject to an additional 20% tax plus interest. See the Instructions for Forms 1040 and 1040-SR.

AA—Designated Roth contributions under a section 401(k) plan

BB—Designated Roth contributions under a section 403(b) plan

DD—Cost of employer-sponsored health coverage. **The amount reported with code DD is not taxable.**

EE—Designated Roth contributions under a governmental section 457(b) plan. This amount does not apply to contributions under a tax-exempt organization section 457(b) plan.

FF—Permitted benefits under a qualified small employer health reimbursement arrangement

GG—Income from qualified equity grants under section 83(i)

HH—Aggregate deferrals under section 83(i) elections as of the close of the calendar year

Box 13. If the "Retirement plan" box is checked, special limits may apply to the amount of traditional IRA contributions you may deduct. See Pub. 590-A, Contributions to Individual Retirement Arrangements (IRAs).

Box 14. Employers may use this box to report information such as state disability insurance taxes withheld, union dues, uniform payments, health insurance premiums deducted, nontaxable income, educational assistance payments, or a member of the clergy's parsonage allowance and utilities. Railroad employers use this box to report railroad retirement (RRTA) compensation, Tier 1 tax, Tier 2 tax, Medicare tax, and Additional Medicare Tax. Include tips reported by the employee to the employer in railroad retirement (RRTA) compensation.

Note: Keep **Copy C** of Form W-2 for at least 3 years after the due date for filing your income tax return. However, to help **protect your social security benefits,** keep Copy C until you begin receiving social security benefits, just in case there is a question about your work record and/or earnings in a particular year.

Department of the Treasury – Internal Revenue Service

NOTE: THESE ARE SUBSTITUTE WAGE AND TAX STATEMENTS AND ARE ACCEPTABLE FOR FILING WITH YOUR FEDERAL, STATE AND LOCAL/CITY INCOME TAX RETURNS.

This information is being furnished to the Internal Revenue Service. If you are required to file a tax return, a negligence penalty or other sanction may be imposed on you if this income is taxable and you fail to report it.

IMPORTANT NOTE:

In order to insure efficient processing, attach this W-2 to your tax return like this (following agency instructions):

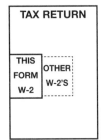

Notice to Employee

Do you have to file? Refer to the Instructions for Forms 1040 and 1040-SR to determine if you are required to file a tax return. Even if you don't have to file a tax return, you may be eligible for a refund if box 2 shows an amount or if you are eligible for any credit.

Earned income credit (EIC). You may be able to take the EIC for 2021 if your adjusted gross income (AGI) is less than a certain amount. The amount of the credit is based on income and family size. Workers without children could qualify for a smaller credit. You and any qualifying children must have valid social security numbers (SSNs). You can't take the EIC if your investment income is more than the specified amount for 2021 or if income is earned for services provided while you were an inmate at a penal institution. For 2021 income limits and more information, visit www.irs.gov/EITC. See also Pub. 596, Earned Income Credit. Any EIC that is more than your tax liability is refunded to you, but only if you file a tax return.

Employee's social security number (SSN). For your protection, this form may show only the last four digits of your SSN. However, your employer has reported your complete SSN to the IRS and SSA.

Clergy and religious workers. If you aren't subject to social security and Medicare taxes, see Pub. 517, Social Security and Other Information for Members of the Clergy and Religious Workers.

Corrections. If your name, SSN, or address is incorrect, correct Copies B, C, and 2 and ask your employer to correct your employment record. Be sure to ask the employer to file Form W-2c, Corrected Wage and Tax Statement, with the Social Security Administration (SSA) to correct any name, SSN, or money amount error reported to the SSA on Form W-2. Be sure to get your copies of Form W-2c from your employer for all corrections made so you may file them with your tax return. If your name and SSN are correct but aren't the same as shown on your social security card, you should ask for a new card that displays your correct name at any SSA office or by calling 800-772-1213. You may also visit the SSA website at www.SSA.gov.

Cost of employer-sponsored health coverage (if such cost is provided by the employer). The reporting in box 12, using code DD, of the cost of employer-sponsored health coverage is for your information only. **The amount reported with code DD is not taxable.**

Credit for excess taxes. If you had more than one employer in 2021 and more than $8,853.60 in social security and/or Tier 1 railroad retirement (RRTA) taxes were withheld, you may be able to claim a credit for the excess against your federal income tax. If you had more than one railroad employer and more than $5,203.80 in Tier 2 RRTA tax was withheld, you may also be able to claim a credit. See the Instructions for Forms 1040 and 1040-SR and Pub. 505, Tax Withholding and Estimated Tax.

Department of the Treasury – Internal Revenue Service

Department of the Treasury – Internal Revenue Service

مربى البندورة

Tomato Jam

2 ½ cups tomatoes, from 3-4 large tomatoes

½ cup (118 ml) water

2 cups (384 g) sugar

1 cup (150 g) dates

¾ cup (127 g) raisins

1 tablespoon (15 g) salt

1 ½ cups (360 ml) red wine vinegar

Cut tomatoes in half, scoop out seeds and discard. Dice the tomatoes and put into a heavy pot with the rest of the ingredients. Bring to a boil and then turn down to a simmer. Stir often and continue to cook on medium-low heat until the jam has thickened, about 45 minutes.

The jam will continue to thicken once cooled. Once completely cooled, store in tightly sealed jars. Jam will keep for several weeks in the refrigerator.

Makes about 5 pints

FAMIL JEAN-CHARLES

Père   Augustin Jean-Charles
Mère   Celicia Bruno

"Fils"

Frantz	Jean-Charles
Rony	Jean-Charles
Olguine	Jean-Charles
Suzette	Jean-Charles
Phariol	Jean-Charles
Jacqueline	Jean-Charles
Robenson	Jean-Charles
Waking	Jean-Charles
Miriame	Jean-Charles
Evens	Jean-Charles
Nadege	Jean-Charles
Fanette	Jean-Charles
Guy Mary	Jean-Charles
Dieuna	Jean-Charles
Ketchna	Jean-Charles
Vanessa	Jean-Charles
Pharison	Jean-Charles
Simon Augustin	Jean-Charles

رقائق زعتر

Sambousek with Za'atar

Dough

4 cups (452 g) whole wheat flour

Pinch of salt

1 teaspoon (5 g) dried yeast

1 teaspoon (5 g) sugar

2 tablespoons (30 g) powdered milk

2 cups (½ liter) lukewarm water, plus more as needed

Filling

2 onions, small diced

1/3 cup (80ml) olive oil

1 bunch of wild za'atar (thyme leaves) chopped, or substitute 1 tablespoon (15 g) dried thyme

1 teaspoon (5 g) fresh lemon juice

Pinch of sumac

Pinch of salt

4 tablespoons olive oil, for brushing

Prepare the dough: In a large mixing bowl, mix together whole wheat flour, salt, yeast, sugar and powdered milk. Slowly add the water while mixing by hand until a ball forms. Knead the ball of dough for about 10 minutes until it becomes smooth and elastic.

Cover the dough loosely and let rest for about an hour.

While the dough rests, prepare the filling: In a large bowl, mix all the ingredients and set aside.

Once the dough has doubled in size, divide into three equal pieces and roll each piece out to a thin sheet about 1/8 inch thick on a clean floured surface.

Cut circles approximately 10 inches in diameter out of the dough. Fill the circles with a few tablespoons of filling, leaving about an inch of space around the edge. Fold over the sides of the dough to form a triangle and pinch or crimp the edges to create a neat seal around the filling.

Preheat oven to 350°F (180°C).

Space evenly on a baking sheet and brush with olive oil. Bake for 15-20 minutes or until golden brown.

Makes about 20

Muhammara

1 cup (112 g) walnuts, finely chopped

1 onion, finely chopped

1 roasted red pepper, finely chopped

1-3 teaspoons (5-15 g) chili flakes or Aleppo pepper

1 ½ tablespoon (20 g) black cumin seeds (nigella seed)

1 tablespoon (15 g) dried oregano

1 tablespoon (15 g) dried coriander

Pinch of salt

1 cup (240 ml) olive oil

1 cup (128 g) walnuts, roughly chopped

Mix all ingredients except walnut pieces by hand in a large bowl. Alternatively, you can pulse all ingredients in a food processor for a smoother texture.

Spread the mixture on a serving plate and top with roughly chopped walnuts and a drizzle with of olive oil. Enjoy with pita or saj bread.

Makes about 4 cups

Pickled Cucumbers

2 cups cucumbers or any other vegetables, washed

1 cup (236 ml) boiling water

3 cups (710 ml) cold water

4 tablespoons (60 g) salt

4 tablespoons (60 ml) white vinegar

Using a toothpick, prick the cucumbers once and add as many as will fit into glass jars. Boil one cup of the water and dissolve the salt in the hot water. Combine the cold water and vinegar, and add the salt water to the cold water to make a brine. Pour the brine over the cucumbers, covering completely. Seal the jars very well, ensuring they are airtight. The pickled cucumbers will be ready in 15 days.

Pickles have a shelf life of approximately 1 year.

Makes about 2 cups

مناقيش بصل وبندورة

Man'oushé with tomatoes and onions

For The Dough

4 cups (480 g) all-purpose flour

2 tablespoons (30 g) powdered milk

1 teaspoon (5 g) salt

1 teaspoon (5 g) sugar

1 tablespoon (15 g) yeast

1/3 cup (80 ml) olive oil

2 cups (472 ml) warm water

For The Topping

½ cup (120 ml) olive oil

3 cups onions, diced, from about 2 onions

3 cups tomatoes, diced, from about 3 tomatoes

Pinch of paprika or chili powder

Pinch of cumin

Pinch of black pepper

Pinch of salt

Prepare the dough: In a mixing bowl, combine flour, milk, salt, sugar and yeast and mix well to combine. Add the oil and mix in with your hands. Add the water intermittently to the mixture as you are mixing it.

Once the mixture has come together evenly, knead it on a counter for 5 minutes until smooth and elastic (add more flour if it's too sticky). Place dough in a clean bowl, cover with a tea towel or cloth and let it rise until it doubles in size, 30-60 minutes.

Make the topping: In a large sauté pan, heat the oil over medium heat and cook onion until soft, 8-10 minutes. Add the tomatoes, chili powder, cumin and black pepper and continue to cook until the tomatoes start to soften and break down, 3-5 minutes. Remove from heat, season to taste with salt and set aside.

Preheat oven to 500°F (260°C).

Divide dough balls into pieces roughly the size of a tennis ball. On a clean floured surface, roll each one into a circle. Arrange on a baking sheet and spread evenly with the tomato-onion mixture.

Bake for about 7 minutes, or until crust is cooked through.

Serves 4-6

Potato Kibbeh

2 cups (300 g) bulgur (cracked wheat)

Pinch of cinnamon

Pinch black pepper

2 pounds (1 kg) potatoes, peeled and cut into quarters

1 pound (½ kg) yellow onion, finely diced

1 pound (½ kg) mozzarella cheese, shredded

Salt to taste

Rinse the bulgur well, then place in a bowl with the cinnamon and black pepper. Leave to sit for 1 to 2 hours, until the bulgur has absorbed all water and doubled in size.

Meanwhile, place the peeled potatoes in a medium pot filled with cold, salted water and bring to a boil. Simmer the potatoes until fork tender, 20-30 minutes. Drain the potatoes, then place in a large bowl and mash them with a ricer, spoon or your hands. Add the onion, cheese, and bulgur mixture and continue to mix with your hands until evenly combined. Season to taste with salt.

Preheat oven to 450°F (230°C).

Using your hands, roll potato mixture into small balls about the size of a golf ball. Mold it into an oval shape with pointed ends.

Place the ovals on a baking sheet and bake for about 20 minutes or until golden brown.

Makes approximately 48 pieces

Molokhia

4 pieces chicken leg
1 cardamom pod
1 cinnamon stick
1 onion, sliced in half lengthwise
5 Swiss chard leaves
1 tablespoon (15 g) butter
1 garlic clove, smashed
1 red chili, diced
1 teaspoon (5 g) coriander
1 pound (½ kg) molokhia (Jute leaves) or substitute 1 pound (½ kg) frozen spinach
Salt to taste

Rinse the chicken and add to a large pot. Fill with water to cover and bring to a boil, regularly skimming the surface. Add cardamom, cinnamon and onion. Simmer until the chicken is cooked through and the meat pulls away easily from the bone, about 45 minutes.

Remove chicken and reserve the broth. When chicken is cool enough to handle, separate the meat from the bone.

Wash, dry and dice the chard leaves, removing the stem.

Heat the butter in a large sauté pan over medium heat. Add the garlic, chili and coriander and cook for 2-3 minutes. Add the molokhia (or spinach), chard and about 2 cups of the reserved chicken broth, and simmer until greens are cooked through. Season to taste with salt.

To serve, stir in the chicken meat to warm through and ladle evenly into bowls.

Serves 4

Chickpea Fatteh

2 cups (400 g) dried chickpeas

Pinch of salt

Pinch of cumin, plus more for garnish

5 cloves garlic, minced, divided

4 cups (908 g) plain full-fat yogurt

1 cup (224 g) tahini

2 pieces saj bread (thin pita bread), toasted until crisp

½ cup toasted pine nuts and cashews to garnish

Soak chickpeas for 24 hours in water and drain.

Simmer together the chickpeas, salt, cumin and half of the garlic with 1 cup of fresh water until chickpeas are very soft, about 1 hour. Drain and add chickpeas to a serving bowl.

While the chickpeas cook, in another pot, mix the yogurt with the tahini, salt, and remaining garlic.

Top the cooked chickpeas with cut pieces of the saj bread, and then cover with the prepared yogurt.

Garnish with more cumin and toasted nuts.

Serves 4

Romanieh

2 cups (280 g) ivory lentil or substitute green lentils

6-8 cups (1 ½-2 liters) of water

1 large eggplant (about 1 pound or 540 g), peeled and cut into cubes

Pinch of salt

2 tablespoons (15 g) all-purpose flour

1 cup (240 ml) unsweetened pomegranate juice

¼ cup (60 ml) oil

10 garlic cloves, minced

1 green pepper, diced small

Toppings

1 pomegranate, seeded

1 lemon, sliced into wedges

Fresh mint and/or thyme

In a large pot, bring lentils and 6 cups of water to a boil. Reduce heat to medium and simmer until lentils are almost cooked through, adding more water if needed. Add the eggplant and salt and continue to cook until the lentils are starting to fall apart.

In a small bowl, mix the flour with the pomegranate juice and add it to the lentils. Warm the oil in a sauté pan and add the garlic and pepper. Cook over medium heat until the garlic starts to turn golden brown, 3-4 minutes. Add to the lentils and stir to combine.

Pour the mixture into a serving bowl or platter while still hot. Top with pomegranate seeds, lemon wedges and mint and/or thyme for presentation. Serve with pita bread or lavash, as an appetizer or as a side dish.

Makes about 5 cups

Tabouli

1 cup (300 g) bulgur (cracked wheat)
½ cup (120 ml) water
Juice of 2 lemons
4 bunches parsley, roughly chopped
1 bunch mint, roughly chopped
4 large onions, finely diced
4 tomatoes, finely diced
½ cup (120ml) olive oil
Salt to taste

Rinse the bulgur well, then place in a bowl with the water and lemon juice. Leave to sit for 1-2 hours, until the bulgur has absorbed all water and doubled in size.

In a large mixing bowl, combine the herbs, onions, tomatoes, and bulgur. Stir well to combine. Add olive oil and salt to taste, and mix well again before serving.

Serves 4

وردة للفريكة (دجاج)

Chicken Freekeh

2 pounds (1 kg) chicken thighs

1 cinnamon stick

2 cardamom cloves

2 bay leaves

1 tablespoon (15 ml) butter

¼ cup (60 ml) neutral oil

1 medium yellow onion, medium diced

2 cups (368 g) freekeh

Pinch of salt

Pinch of white pepper

Pinch of ground cardamom

2 teaspoons (10 g) ground ginger

1 cup (100 g) chopped almonds, for garnish

Place chicken thighs, cinnamon stick, cardamom cloves and bay leaves in a large pot and fill with water to cover. Bring to a boil, then reduce heat and simmer until the chicken is cooked through and the meat pulls away easily from the bone. Remove the thighs from the pot and reserve the cooking liquid. When chicken is cool enough to handle, shred it by hand and set aside.

Warm the oil and butter in a pot and add the diced onion. Saute over medium heat until the onion becomes soft. Add the freekeh, salt, pepper, ground cardamom and ground ginger. Stir and cook for 2 minutes. Add 5 cups of the liquid the chicken was cooked in. Stir and cook until the water is all gone. (About 20 minutes if you are using cracked freekeh and 45 minutes if you are using whole berry freekeh).

To serve, arrange the shredded chicken on top of the freekeh along with the almonds.

Alternate Serving Option:
Using one sheet of markouk bread, add the mixture to the center, pull the sides up and using a long narrow strip cut from the edge of the bread, tie it around the top to create a pouch.

Serves 5

منسف دجاج

Chicken Mansaf

1 cinnamon stick

3 cardamom pods

3 whole cloves

2 bay leaves

1 whole nutmeg

4 pounds (2 kg) chicken thighs

1 tablespoon (15 g) butter

¼ cup (60 ml) oil

2 cups (400 g) long grain rice

2 pinches of salt

Pinch of allspice

Pinch of black pepper

¾ cup roasted nuts for garnish (such as pine nuts and/or almonds)

Note: Palestinians in Lebanon, specifically in the refugee camps, do not add yogurt to their Mansaf.

In a large pot, combine cinnamon, cardamom, cloves, bay leaves, nutmeg, a pinch of salt and chicken thighs and add water to cover. Simmer for about 30 minutes or until chicken is cooked through and pulls easily from the bone. Remove the chicken and set aside. Strain spices from the broth and discard, but save the liquid. Once the chicken is cool enough to handle, cut into medium-sized pieces and set aside.

Put the butter and oil in the large pot over medium heat and add the rice, stirring for 2 minutes. Add 4 cups of the reserved chicken broth, another pinch of salt, allspice and black pepper. Stir and bring to a boil. Reduce heat to a simmer and cook for 20-30 minutes, or until the rice has absorbed all of the liquid.

Arrange rice on a platter and top with chicken and roasted nuts.

Serves 5

منسف لحمة

Meat Mansaf

1 cinnamon stick

3 cardamom pods

3 whole cloves

2 bay leaves

1 whole nutmeg

1 pound (½ kg) lamb or beef stew meat, cubed

1 tablespoon (15 g) butter

¼ cup (60 ml) oil

2 cups (400 g) long grain rice

2 pinches of salt

Pinch of allspice

Pinch of black pepper

½ pound (¼ kg) ground beef (optional)

2 tablespoons olive oil (if using ground beef)

¾ cup roasted nuts for garnish (such as pine nuts and/or almonds)

Note: Palestinians in Lebanon, specifically in the refugee camps, do not add yogurt to their Mansaf.

Toss the meat cubes with 1 pinch of salt and add to a large pot with the cinnamon stick, cardamom, cloves, bay leaves and nutmeg. Cover with water and simmer until meat is tender, about 1 hour. Remove the meat and set aside. Strain spices from the broth and discard, but save the liquid.

Put the butter and oil in the large pot over medium heat and add the rice, stirring for 2 minutes. Add 4 cups of the reserved broth, another pinch of salt, allspice and black pepper. Stir and bring to a boil. Reduce heat to a simmer and cook for 20-30 minutes, or until the rice has absorbed all of the liquid.

If using ground beef: Heat a small sauté pan with the olive oil over medium heat. Add the ground beef and cook, stirring often to break up clumps, until cooked through. Season with salt and pepper.

Arrange rice on a platter and top with cubed meat, ground meat if using, and roasted nuts.

Serves 5

قدرة بالفخار

Qidra

For The Meat

2 pounds (1 kg) lamb or beef stew meat, cut into large cubes

1 tablespoon salt

1 carrot, diced large

1 onion, diced large

1 garlic clove

1 bay leaf

For The Rice

½ cup (120 g) vegetable oil

2 cups sliced carrots

2 onions, finely diced

4 garlic cloves, minced

2 cups (480 g) cooked chickpeas

2 cubes chicken bouillon

1 tablespoon (15 g) caraway seeds

1 teaspoon (5 g) mixed spice: blend of ¼ teaspoon each ginger, cinnamon, black pepper and cardamom

2 cups (400 g) long-grain rice

Salt to taste

Prepare the meat: Toss the meat with salt and put in a large pot along with carrot, onion, garlic and bay leaf. Cover with water and bring to a boil, then reduce heat to a simmer and cook 1 hour, or until meat is tender and cooked through. Skim any impurities off the top as the meat simmers. Strain the meat and set aside. Discard the vegetables and bay leaf but save the cooking liquid.

In a large pot, heat oil over medium heat. Add carrots and onions and cook, stirring often, until soft and caramelized, about 12-15 minutes. Add the garlic and stir for another 3-4 minutes. Add the chickpeas, then the chicken bouillon, caraway and mixed spice. Add the rice and stir for 2 minutes. Add the meat and 4 cups of the cooking liquid. Add water if there isn't enough juice from meat to make 4 cups, and season to taste with salt.

Bring to a boil, lower heat to a simmer and cover. Cook for 45 minutes, or until rice has absorbed all of the liquid, and serve.

Serves 6-8

Wheatberry Porridge

2 cups (370 g) wheat berries, or substitute farro

Sugar to taste

Orange blossom water (optional)

½ cup (65 g) walnuts, chopped

½ cup (70 g) almonds, chopped

½ cup (75 g) raisins

1 pomegranate, seeded

½ cup (40 g) unsweetened coconut flakes

Rinse the wheat berries well in water, then drain. Place in a large heavy saucepan, cover with 4 cups of water and cook over medium heat for about an hour, or until wheat berries have softened and absorbed all water. Add more water if necessary.

Once cooked, stir in the sugar and orange blossom water, if using.

Divide the porridge into individual serving bowls, and top with walnuts, almonds, raisins, pomegranate seeds, and coconut as desired. Serve warm.

Makes about 8 cups

Safeye Naser — "I am Lebanese from Beqaa Valley. One of my favorite childhood memories was my mother feeding me handmade kibbeh. My favorite spice is Za'atar."

صفيه ناصر أنا لبنانية من وادي البقاع. من ذكريات طفولتي أن والدتي كانت تطعمني الكبّة المصنوعة يدوياً. و أكثر شيء أحبه هو الزعتر.

Samar Hanafi — "I love working with dough, chocolate and patisseries, and am really great at making jams."

سمر حنفي أحبّ العمل مع العجين والشوكولاتة والحلويات، وأنا ماهرة جداً في صنع المربّيات.

Manal Hasan — "I remember the aromas of my mother and grandmother cooking. Cooking for others makes me happy, it doesn't feel like work."

منال حسن أتذكر رائحة طبخ أمي وجدتي. إن الطبخ للآخرين يجعلني سعيدة، ولا أشعر أنه مجرد عمل.

Maha Hajjaj — "I like learning new recipes of other women, and I remember cooking with my mother when I was young. I really love cinnamon."

مها حجاج أحب تعلّم وصفات جديدة من نساء أخريات، وأتذكر الطبخ مع أمي عندما كنت شابّة. أنا أحب القرفة كثيراً.

Nehmat Al Zoghbi — "I am from Syria and I love Palestinian food and I'm so happy to be part of the Soufra team. One of my favorite Palestinian dishes is Freekeh with meat, and my favorite spices are black pepper and ginger."

نعمة الزعبي انا من سوريا واحب الاكل الفلسطيني وانا سعيدة جدا بالانضمام الى مطبخ سفرة. من اكلاتي المفضلة الفريكة على لحمة وبالنسبة للبهارات فلفل اسود والزنجبيل .

Zeinab Jammal — "I enjoy the aroma of the Palestinian dishes, and I particularly love cinnamon."

زينب جمال أستمتع برائحة الأطباق الفلسطينية، وبالذات أنا أحبّ القرفة.

Sweet

Samar Shaar — "My favorites are the Mansaf with Chicken, and strawberry tarte. My favorite seasoning is the spiciness of black pepper."

سمر شعار أطباقي المفضّلة هي المنسف مع الدجاج، وتارت الفراولة. أما التوابل المفضلة لديّ فهي توابل الفلفل الأسود.

Maakaroun

For Dough

4 cups (480 g) all-purpose flour

1 cup (168 g) semolina flour

1 cup (192 g) sugar

1 teaspoon (5 ml) baking powder

3 tablespoons (45 g) ground anise seed

1 tablespoon (15 g) mahlab, or substitute

1 teaspoon (5ml) almond extract

1 ½ (339 g) cups butter, cut into 1-inch pieces

1 cup (236 ml) water

1 quart vegetable oil for frying, plus more as needed

For Sugar Syrup

4 cups (768 g) sugar

2 cups (472 ml) water

1 teaspoon (5 ml) lemon juice

1 tablespoon (15 ml) rosewater

Prepare the dough: In a large mixing bowl, combine both flours, sugar, baking powder and anise seed. Mix the mahlab and butter in with your hands until well incorporated. Add the water and continue to mix by hand until a ball forms. Cover and let the dough rest for 30 minutes.

Cut the dough into finger-shaped pieces, then decorate with a fork or press into the edge of a cheese grater or colander, and set aside on a tray.

Make the sugar syrup: Bring sugar, water, and lemon juice together to a boil. Add the rosewater and boil for an additional 2 minutes, then set aside.

Heat the oil in a large, heavy-bottomed pot with tall walls until it reaches 365°F (185°C). Working in batches to avoid overcrowding, fry the dough carefully until light brown, about 3-5 minutes. Remove from oil and dip in sugar syrup, then set aside on a paper-towel lined cooling rack.

Makes about 70 pieces

كنافة نابلسية

Knafeh Nabulsieh

Pie

1 pound (½ kg) othmaliye (shredded phyllo) dough

8 ounces (226 g) melted butter

1 pound (453 g) whole milk ricotta

1 cup chopped pistachios, toasted

Ingredients For Sugar Water

1 cup (236 ml) water

1 cup (194 g) sugar

1 tablespoon (15 ml) orange blossom water (optional)

Juice of one lemon

In a large mixing bowl, crumble the othmaliye into smaller pieces with your hands. Pour the melted butter over the dough and mix well with your hands to make sure it is completely coated with butter.

Spread out half the othmaliye dough on a greased pizza pan or large pie pan. Gently spread the ricotta over the dough, spreading to the edges, then cover with the remaining dough. Bake for 35-45 minutes, or until the dough is golden brown.

To prepare the sugar water, place the sugar and water in a saucepan and bring to a boil for 5 minutes. Remove from heat and add lemon juice and orange blossom water, if using. Stir well.

Let pie cool in the pan for 10 minutes before flipping it out onto a serving platter or cake stand. Pour the sugar water over it as desired and top with chopped pistachios.

Serves 6-8

كعك الدبس

Molasses Cookies

4 cup (480 g) corn flour
1 cup (120 g) self-rising flour
1 tablespoon (15 g) baking powder
1 tablespoon (15 g) ground anise seeds
½ cup (120 ml) vegetable oil
½ cup (120 ml) olive oil
1 cup (340 g) molasses
2 tablespoons (30 g) sesame seeds

Preheat oven to 350°F (180°C).

In a large mixing bowl, mix together both flours, baking powder and anise seeds. Make a well in the middle then add both oils and molasses, and slowly mix together to form a dough ball. Chill for 15-20 minutes in the refrigerator to make it easier to roll.

On a clean surface, roll out the dough evenly into a sheet about ¼ inch thick, then use a round cookie cutter to cut as many circles as possible.

Line a baking sheet with parchment or oil to avoid sticking, and arrange cookies on top. Sprinkle with sesame seeds and bake for 7-10 minutes, or until golden. Allow to cool completely.

Alternate presentation: Roll the cut dough circles into a tube shape, sticking the edges together, then roll into sesame seeds and bake.

Recipe makes about 50 cookies

كرات الشوكولا

Chocolate Balls

4 cups (568g) finely ground digestive biscuits, such as McVities Digestives or substitute Graham crackers

One 14 ounce-can (397g) sweetened condensed milk or 2 cups (640g) fruit-flavored jam

1 tablespoon (15ml) cocoa powder (omit if using jam)

1 cup chocolate sprinkles, rainbow sprinkles, ground pistachios, powdered sugar, and/or shredded coconut for decoration

In a food processor or blender, pulse the biscuits into a rough-ground powder. Add the condensed milk or jam and cocoa powder (if using) and pulse again until mixture is well-blended and uniform.

Using your hands, divide the mixture into small balls about the size of a ping-pong ball. If necessary, put a little bit of the condensed milk on your palms while rolling the balls to keep them from sticking.

Roll the balls in sprinkles, ground pistachios, powdered sugar, and/or shredded coconut. Refrigerate until firm.

Makes approximately 40 cookies

مقروطة

Makrouta

2 cups (240 g) all-purpose flour

2 cups (336 g) semolina flour

1 pinch dry yeast

1 teaspoon (5 ml) ground anise seed

1 teaspoon (5 ml) mahlab, or substitute ½ teaspoon (2.5 ml) almond extract

1 ½ cups (339 g) butter

Water, as needed

1 pound (30 g) date paste

1 cup (142 g) sesame seeds

1 cup (113 g) powdered sugar

Preheat the oven to 350°F (180°C).

Mix both flours, yeast, anise, mahlab and butter together. Mix by hand until butter forms into small pieces. If the dough is not easily forming into a ball, add a little water, 1 tablespoon at a time, until it comes together. Chill in the refrigerator for 15 minutes.

Roll out the dough into a sheet about ¼ inch thick on a clean surface. Spread a thick layer of date paste evenly to the edges, then roll the dough into a log over the paste. Sprinkle sesame seeds on top and cut into two-inch pieces.

Arrange on a baking sheet and bake for about 15 minutes, until golden brown. Remove from oven and immediately sprinkle with powdered sugar while the pastries are still hot.

Makes about 24 pieces

نمورة جوز الهند

Coconut Namoura

2½ cups (282 g) unsweetened coconut flakes

½ cups (96 g) sugar

1 cup (168 g) fine semolina flour

½ cup (114 g) plain full-fat Greek yogurt

2 eggs

2 tablespoons (30 g) vegetable oil

½ cup (60 g) all-purpose flour

2 teaspoons (10 ml) vanilla extract

1 teaspoon (5 g) baking powder

For Sugar Syrup

2 cups (192 g) sugar

1 cup (236 ml) water

1 tablespoon (15 ml) orange blossom water

Juice of one lemon

For the cake: Preheat oven to 350°F or 180°C and grease a 9-inch square baking pan.

In a large mixing bowl, combine all ingredients and mix until batter is uniform. Pour the batter into the greased baking pan and bake until golden brown and set, about 30 minutes.

While the cake bakes, make the sugar syrup: Place the sugar and water into a small saucepan and bring to a boil. Remove from heat and stir in the lemon juice and the orange blossom water.

Once the cake is baked through, remove from oven and while still hot, pour the sugar syrup evenly on top and leave to cool in the pan. The sugar water will be absorbed into the cake. Once cool, cut into squares and serve.

Makes about 30 squares

تارت الفريز

Strawberry Tart

For The Dough

1 cup (192 g) sugar

1 cup (226 g) butter, at room temperature

2 eggs

Zest of 2 lemons

1 teaspoon (5 ml) vanilla extract

3 cups (360 g) all-purpose flour

For The Patissiere Crème Filling

¼ cup (32 g) cornstarch

½ cup (96 g) sugar

Zest of 1 lemon

4 eggs

4 cups (1 liter) water

½ cup (80 g) powdered milk

For Decoration

Sliced kiwi

Sliced strawberry

Sliced pineapple

Unflavored gelatin for glazing fruit (optional)

The Dough

Mix sugar and butter by hand or with the help of a mixer until creamed. Add the eggs one at a time with the lemon zest and vanilla. When all of these ingredients are well incorporated, add the flour all at once and mix just until all of the flour is incorporated, being careful not to overwork the dough. Wrap the dough in plastic and chill in the refrigerator for 30 minutes.

Preheat the oven to 350°F (180°C).

Roll out half of the dough or hand press it into a fluted tart pan, spreading the dough evenly into the edges. If you have a second tart pan you can make another tarts with the second half of the dough, or wrap the second half and reserve for another tart or pie in the future.

To prevent the dough from forming bubbles, prick with a fork all over.

Bake for 18 minutes or until lightly browned. Once done, allow to cool, then cover and refrigerate. The pastry shells can be saved for a second day or used immediately.

The Patissiere Crème Filling

In a bowl, mix the cornstarch, sugar, lemon zest and eggs together and beat well with an electric mixer until creamy.

In a pot, heat the water and powdered milk over medium heat and bring to a boil. Remove the pot from the heat and slowly pour half of the hot liquid into the bowl with the egg mixture, whisking the eggs as the milk is added to avoid curdling.

Pour everything back into the pot and return to medium-low heat, stirring constantly. As soon as small bubbles start to form, immediately pour the hot mixture into a clean bowl. Stir in the vanilla and let cool. Cover and refrigerate.

To assemble, pour the cooled crème filling into the tart shells. Decorate with sliced fruit, and glaze with gelatin to preserve, if desired.

Makes two 9-inch tarts

مربى الاناناس

Pineapple Jam

1 medium pineapple
3 tablespoons (45 ml) water
1 teaspoon (5 g) salt
Juice of one lemon
2 cups (384 g) sugar

Peel and dice the pineapple, being sure to remove the hard core. Place the chopped pineapple into a heavy pot with the water, salt and lemon juice and simmer low heat. When the mix has started to soften, add the sugar, keeping on low heat and stirring often. Cook until the sugar and pineapple mix has thickened, approximately 30 minutes. Cool completely before storing tightly in jars.

Makes about 4 pints

Manal Faour — "I am from Syria and I love freekeh. I remember all the beautiful aromas in the kitchen when I was a child. Sumac is delicious, and I really enjoy coming to the kitchen with the other women and learning about Palestinian dishes."

منال فأعور أنا من سوريا وأحب الفريكه. أتذكر كل الروائح الجميلة في المطبخ عندما كنت طفلة. السمّاق لذيذ، وأنا أحبّ فعلاً أن آتي إلى المطبخ مع النساء الأخريات وأن أتعلّم عن الأطباق الفلسطينية.

Maysaa Hussein — "Mansaf with meat is one of my favorite dishes, and among the spices I love cinnamon."

ميساء حسين من افضل الاطباق لدي هو المنسف على لحمة ومن البهارات احب القرفة

Ameera Fnesh — "My favorite flavor is that of cumin. I remember living in the countryside as child and cooking with ingredients picked fresh from the land."

أميرة فنيش الأفضل لدي هي نكهة الكمّون. أتذكر كيف كنت أعيش في الريف كطفلة وكيف كنا نطبخ باستخدام مكونات نأخذها طازجة من الأرض.

Khadija Abou Hassan — "I am Palestinian married to a Lebanese man, and I am a widow. Being part of Soufra gives me so much happiness. My favorite dishes are stuffed grape leaves, and my favorite spice is cumin."

خديجة ابو حسان انا فلسطينية متزوجة رجل لبناني وانا ارملة سعيدة بالانضمام لمطبخ سفرة ومن اكلاتي المفضلة ورق العنب وبالنسبة للبهارات احب الكمون .

Randa Abbas — "I love cinnamon in my tea, and I enjoy learning new recipes with the women in the kitchen."

رندة عباس أحبّ القرفة في الشاي، وأحب أن أتعلّم وصفات جديدة مع النساء في المطبخ.

Bourj el-Barajneh

Aley, Lebanon
Hills above Beirut

Acknowledgements

Rebelhouse is deeply grateful to Craig Piligian and the many good people of Pilgrim Media Group who believed in the women of Soufra enough to put their considerable support, and heart, behind our film and this cookbook. Thanks are also due to Jessie Creel and Anderson Hinsch of Old Mill Ventures, and Barry Landry and Sarah Gauger who all believed in us and provided support long before we could see the finish line. Underneath it all were Rebelhouse's most loyal partners, Cara Casey Hall and Jenny Bonk, who provided endless guidance and a steady dose of love. We must also recognize the many talented Soufra filmmakers, advisors, and contributors, including: Kathleen Glynn, Susan Sarandon, Claudia Carasso, Lisa Madison, Teresa Chahine, Michelle Mouracade, Sarba Das, Jenelle Lindsay, Claire Hamady, Kelly Kopchik, Lauren Thompson, Mohamed El Manasterly, Ibrahim Nada, Barbara Vick, Daisy Mohr, Johny Karam, Myrna Atalla, Reem Al Rasheed, Nicole Guillemet, The Elgouna Film Festival, Ron Schneider, Vicki Kennedy, Bill Rossi, Jenny Haines, Ginger Tolman and Suzanne Lerner. Finally, we must give our most heartfelt gratitude and praise for the one women who gracefully took the lead on every element of this book, Gretchen Thomas. Without Gretchen and the women of Soufra, this book simply would not exist.